SECRETS OF Magic

CLOSE-UP TRICKS

STEPHANIE TURNBULL

A+

Smart Apple Media

Published by Smart Apple Media
P.O. Box 3263
Mankato, MN 56002

Printed in the United States of America at Corporate Graphics, in North Mankato, Minnesota.

Library of Congress Cataloging-in-Publication Data
Turnbull, Stephanie.
 Close-up tricks / Stephanie Turnbull.
    p. cm. -- (Secrets of magic)
 Includes index.
 ISBN 978-1-59920-496-3 (library binding)
 1. Magic tricks--Juvenile literature. I. Title.
 GV1548.T85 2012
 793.8--dc22

                                                             2011000252

Created by Appleseed Editions, Ltd.
Designed and illustrated by Guy Callaby
Edited by Mary-Jane Wilkins
Picture research by Su Alexander

Picture credits
l = left, r = right, t = top, b = bottom
Contents page Eline Spek/Shutterstock; 4t Roberto Cerutti/Shutterstock, b Vehbi Koca/Alamy; 6 Dhannte/Shutterstock; 7 Trinacria Photo/Shutterstock; 8 Tatiana Popover/Shutterstock; 10 Bernd Vogel/Corbis; 12 Koh Sze Kiat/Shutterstock; 14 Vadim Kozlovsky/Shutterstock; 15 AFP/ Getty Images; 16 Scott Richardson/Shutterstock; 17 Time & Life Pictures/Getty Images; 18t Matthew Cole/Shutterstock, b Drozdowski/Shutterstock; 20 HD Connelly/Shutterstock; 22 Lena Lir/Shutterstock; 24 EP_Stock/Shutterstock; 26 Bernd Vogel/Corbis; 28 Stephen Coburn/Shutterstock
Front Cover: Gelpi/Shutterstock

DAD0049D
2-2012

9 8 7 6 5 4 3 2

Contents

4 Watch Very Closely . . .

6 Tricks of the Trade

8 Card Magic

10 Coin Magic

12 Clever Coin Moves

14 Big Money Tricks

16 Dice Magic

18 Cups and Balls

20 Rubber Bands

22 Amazing Matches

24 Mealtime Magic

26 Fun with Food

28 Show Time!

30 Glossary

31 Web Sites

32 Index

Watch Very Closely...

IF YOU WANT to become a magician, try learning close-up tricks. They're quick, slick, and perfect for amazing your friends. You don't need a stage or a big audience—close-up tricks are best performed for a small group or even just one person, and all your **props** will fit in your pocket!

TABLE AND STREET MAGIC

Some magicians perform close-up magic for small groups of people at tables—for example, in a restaurant. Other close-up magicians prefer **street magic**. This involves doing tricks outside in a park or on a street corner. Another method is to approach unsuspecting passersby and surprise them with just one or two tricks. This is called guerrilla magic and is popular on TV shows.

Many street magicians do card tricks. Cards are easy to carry around and perfect for small, close-up audiences.

CLOSE-UP PROPS

Close-up magic uses simple, everyday props such as playing cards, coins, bills, rubber bands, matches, and dice. If you're performing at a dinner table, you can include objects such as cups, napkins, or even food. The great thing about these props is that the audience knows they're ordinary items without any **gimmicks**, which makes the magic even more astonishing!

TYPES OF TRICKS

Many tricks involve **sleight-of-hand**—in other words, sneaky moves your audience doesn't notice. Many sleight-of-hand tricks take years to perfect. Other tricks work automatically as long as you follow the instructions exactly. This book contains examples of each type for you to try.

TRICK OF THE TRADE
Whenever you can, borrow props from your audience to perform tricks. That way they'll know there are no hidden gimmicks.

SLYDINI (1900–1991)

The Italian magician Tony Slydini was one of the most skillful close-up performers ever. He began his career as a stage magician. He was fascinated by the idea that he could do a trick for people who were standing right next to him that still couldn't see how the trick was done! He decided to perform just close-up magic, which was very unusual at the time, but he did it so well that soon other magicians were copying his style—and many still do today.

Tricks of the Trade

THE KEY TO becoming a great close-up magician is to remember three Ps: practice, **patter**, and performance. Practice always comes first. You should practice each trick until you can do it quickly, easily, and confidently. Then you're ready to work on your patter—in other words, what you say—and your performance style.

MISDIRECTION SKILLS

At first you may feel nervous about doing tricks so close to people. They're bound to spot what you're up to, right? Wrong! Remember that they have no idea what you're going to do, and because they're so close to you, they can't see everything at once. If you distract them with patter, then they'll miss any sneaky moves you're making. This is called **misdirection**.

By pointing to his right fist, this magician misdirects attention from his left hand, where he may have something hidden!

Look! The match is whole again!

If you tell people to look at or concentrate on something, then they'll do as they're told! Just make sure you look at it too and not the thing you're trying to hide.

TRICK OF THE TRADE
Never repeat a trick for the same audience. They'll be watching much more closely, so your misdirection patter and moves will be less effective.

SMOOTH MOVES

Everyone will be watching your hands, so handle props smoothly and gracefully. This makes your performance look more professional, and it helps with misdirection too. For example, a wave or **flourish** of one hand can distract the audience from what the other hand is doing. You can read more performance tips on page 28–29.

Magicians often wave wands to help misdirect the audience's attention. It can also make their act look more exciting.

MAGIC LINKING PAPER CLIPS

Here's a quick trick to get you started which doesn't involve tricky sleight-of-hand. Try it on a friend.

1. Take a strip of paper and fold it lengthwise to strengthen it.

2. Now fold it into the shape of a "z," like this.

3. Clip one paper clip to the back and middle sections of the "z" and an identical paper clip to the middle and front sections.

4. Hold the paper by the ends. Say a magic word and pull the ends apart sharply. The paper clips will jump into the air and join together as they jump!

The harder you pull, the higher the paper clips will spring.

MAX MALINI
(1873–1942)

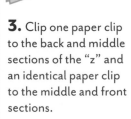

*The Polish magician Max Malini was an expert at close-up magic with coins, cards, and other small props. He was so successful that he performed for U.S. presidents and the British royal family. Malini achieved success despite one big disadvantage—he had tiny hands. His hands were so small that he couldn't **palm** a card properly, but Malini never let this stop him from doing magic. He devised his own clever moves and imaginative effects and became a master of misdirection techniques that even fooled other magicians. For example, he put a coin under a hat and then lifted the hat to reveal a huge block of ice. No one ever figured out how he did it!*

Card Magic

ALL GOOD CLOSE-UP magicians need a few card tricks up their sleeves. Here are some essential card skills, plus a great trick to get you started. You'll find many more card tricks in another book in this series, *Secrets of Magic: Card Tricks.*

*Buy a good quality **deck** of cards with plastic coating—they will be smooth and easy to handle and will last a long time.*

CRAFTY CUTTING

All magicians need to know how to **cut** a deck of cards. You can use it to find someone's card.

1. First, sneak a peek at the bottom card as you pick up the deck.

Remember this card!

2. Put the deck on the table and ask a friend to look at the top card without showing it to you. Then replace it.

3. Now cut the deck. This means taking a chunk of cards off the top, placing them on the table . . .

. . . then putting the rest of the deck on top.

4. Cut the deck several times, or ask your friend to do it. Then fan out the deck in your hands. Your friend's card will always be to the right of the one you know.

SNEAKY SHUFFLING

You must also be able to **shuffle**. Here's how you can use shuffling to identify a card.

1. Hold the deck in your right hand and rest it on your left (or the other way around if you're left-handed). Lift most of the deck, and then drop a few cards in front of and behind the cards in your left hand. Keep going until all the cards are together again. This is called a straight shuffle.

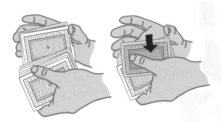

2. Sneak a peek at the bottom card.

3. Shuffle the cards again, but this time drop the final card on its own on top of the deck. This is called a false shuffle.

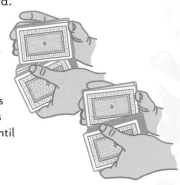

4. Now offer the top card to a friend to look at and replace. Although it looks as though the deck was properly shuffled, you know exactly what they picked!

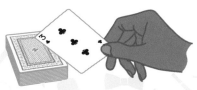

5. Do straight shuffle or two, fan out the cards, and produce the card your friend chose.

JUMPING JACKS

1. Beforehand, pull out the four jacks from a deck of cards plus three extra cards. Put the three cards facedown in your hand and the jacks faceup on top.

It doesn't matter what these cards are.

2. Fan out the cards on the table and tell the audience you've removed the jacks. Show them, but hold them with your hand tilted downward, so no one sees you're holding three extra cards.

3. Prove you're holding all four jacks by pulling them out one at a time and then replacing them facedown at the back of the pile.

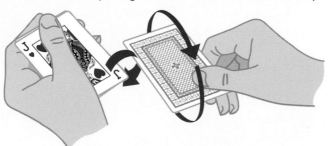

4. Put the deck in a pile, facedown, and place the cards from your hand on top.

5. Tell the audience you'll move the jacks around. Take the top card and slide it into the deck near the bottom. Put the next card near the middle and the next card near the top.

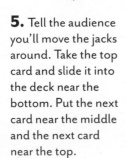

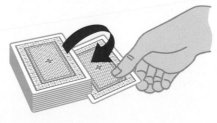

The audience thinks you're moving jacks, when in fact these are random cards, so be careful to keep them facedown.

6. Say you'll leave the last jack on top, and turn it over briefly to show it's a jack.

7. Now say that you can make the jacks jump back to the top. Tap the deck, or snap your fingers, and then slowly and dramatically turn over the top four cards—the jacks are back together!

9

Coin Magic

COINS ARE PERFECT props for magic, and many great close-up magicians use them. Here are a few clever coin tricks which are easy to learn. Once you've mastered these, turn the page and try some trickier moves.

THE SHRINKING COIN

This trick is easy, but practice until you can do it smoothly. The faster you perform the last step, the more impressive it will be.

1. Draw around a small coin, such as a dime or penny, on a piece of paper.

2. Cut out the circle carefully so you're left with a hole in the paper. Show that the coin can drop through the hole.

3. Now take a bigger coin, such as a nickel or quarter, and challenge someone to make it drop through without tearing the hole.

4. When they give up, take the paper and fold it across the middle of the hole. Put the big coin inside the fold.

5. Hold the paper near the fold and push the sides up and into the middle. The paper will buckle outward, letting the coin slip through the hole.

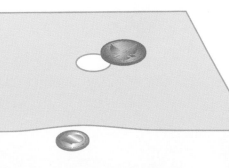

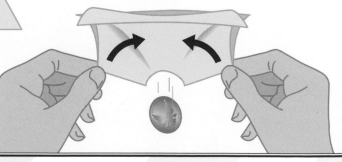

X-Ray Vision

Unlike most tricks, you can do this one again and again. It's more effective if you repeat it, so people don't think you just got lucky the first time.

1. Ask someone to put a handful of coins on a table. Quickly look to see whether there is an odd or even number of heads.

2. Turn away so you can't see the coins. Ask the person to turn over two coins at a time as many times as they like.

3. Now ask them to cover one coin. Say you'll be able to see through their hand and tell them which side faces upward —heads or tails.

To do this, quickly scan the coins again to see if there is an odd or even number. If this is the same as before (still odd or still even), then the hidden coin is tail up. If it has changed (from odd to even or even to odd), then it's head up.

4. Stare hard at the person's hand as if you're seeing through it, and then announce the correct answer!

Heads!

Jumping Coins

With practice, this is easier than you think.

1. Place a coin in the middle of your left palm and another on the right side of your right palm. Show the audience you have a coin in each hand.

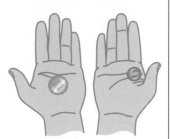

2. Lay your hands palm-up on the table, and then quickly turn your hands over. The coin in your right palm should jump across to your left hand.

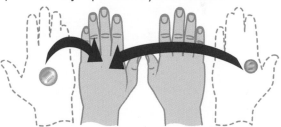

3. Say, "So I've got a coin under each hand, right? Wrong!" Lift your hands to show both coins under your left hand!

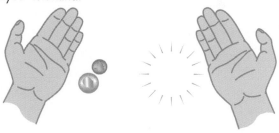

4. Now try swapping two coins. To do this, place both coins on the sides of your palms. Ask a volunteer to remember which hand each coin is in.

5. Quickly slap your hands over so that each coin jumps to the other hand. Ask the volunteer to remind you which coin is where. Lift your hands to show them they're wrong!

TRICK OF THE TRADE
Do this trick on a tablecloth to muffle the sound of the coins and stop them from rolling.

Clever Coin Moves

MASTER MAGICIANS HOLD coins in many clever ways so their hands look empty. They then make the coins appear out of thin air or from someone's pocket or ear! The problem is that moves like this take years to perfect. Here are a few simpler sleights to try.

FINGER PALMING

One way of hiding a coin in your hand is a finger palm. You bend your two middle fingers to hold the coin in place. Then remember two things: first, hold your hand naturally. Second, misdirect the audience's attention by doing something interesting with your other hand!

BREAD ROLL SURPRISE

Try performing this in a restaurant or when you're eating at a friend's house.

1. Hide a coin in one hand using a finger palm. Use the highest value coin you have.

2. Pick up a bread roll with your other hand and grab attention by staring at it and shaking it next to your ear.

3. Hold the roll with both hands, thumbs on top and the coin hidden underneath. Press down into the middle to break the roll open underneath, and secretly push the coin into the crack.

View from underneath

4. Now push up on the roll so the top breaks open and the coin is pushed farther up inside.

Keep the pieces of roll together at the bottom so the coin doesn't fall out.

5. Say, "I don't believe this . . . look!" Reach into the roll and pull out the coin.

MULTIPLY YOUR MONEY

This only works if the angle of your hand is exactly right.
Do lots of practice in front of a mirror!

1. Before you show this trick, put your coins in position. Grip a nickel between your thumb and index finger and hold a penny at right angles in front of it, like this.

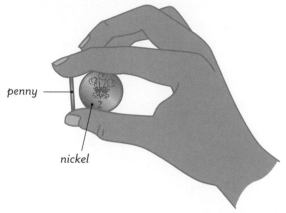

penny

nickel

2. Show the penny to a friend sitting opposite. Say that you can magically multiply it.

This is your friend's view. The big coin is hidden.

3. Show that your other hand is empty, and then bring it over to take the coin. As you do this, push the penny with your thumb so it turns to rest against the nickel.

penny behind nickel

4. Now hold up the nickel with the penny hidden behind it. The coin has magically multiplied!

Magician's view

TRICK OF THE TRADE

Practice step 3 until you can do it smoothly, or the coins will clink and give away the secret. You could also play music when you perform to mask any sounds.

MASTER MAGICIAN

THOMAS NELSON DOWNS (1867–1938)

Thomas Nelson Downs is probably the most famous coin magician ever. He was an expert in coin sleights by the age of 12 and went on to perform across the U.S. and Europe, calling himself the "King of Koins." Although it was unusual at the time to perform only coin magic, Downs was a huge success because he was so inventive. One of his best-known effects was called The Miser's Dream. It involved pulling coin after coin out of thin air. Downs did this by palming coins in his hand and revealing them one by one. He used specially-made, thin coins and palmed as many as 60 in one hand.

Big Money Tricks

WHY NOT TRY some tricks with paper money too? These can be fun, especially if you borrow the money from your audience. They'll be on the edge of their seats, hoping their money is returned to them safely!

TURNING MONEY ON ITS HEAD

This trick works with any bill which has an obvious face or figure on it.

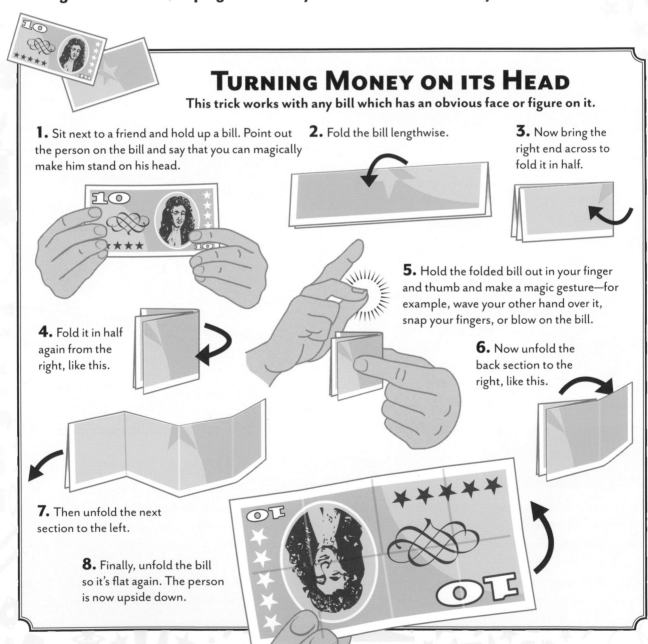

1. Sit next to a friend and hold up a bill. Point out the person on the bill and say that you can magically make him stand on his head.

2. Fold the bill lengthwise.

3. Now bring the right end across to fold it in half.

4. Fold it in half again from the right, like this.

5. Hold the folded bill out in your finger and thumb and make a magic gesture—for example, wave your other hand over it, snap your fingers, or blow on the bill.

6. Now unfold the back section to the right, like this.

7. Then unfold the next section to the left.

8. Finally, unfold the bill so it's flat again. The person is now upside down.

TRICK OF THE TRADE
Make this into a game by saying that if anyone can free the bill, they'll win it. Of course you'll end up pocketing the cash!

THE TRAPPED BILL

All you need for this is a bill, some coins, and a bottle.
Make sure the coins are bigger than the opening of the bottle.

1. Put a bottle on the table and lie the bill on top of it. You may have to crease it slightly so it sticks straight out. Pile four coins on top of the bill, over the top of the bottle.

2. Challenge your friends to take the bill from under the coins without knocking any coins off. They won't be able to!

3. Now show them how it's done. Make a big deal of flexing your hand to warm up, and then hold your index finger straight and suddenly karate chop the bill.

4. If you do this quickly and firmly enough, the bill will fall out, leaving the coins balanced on top of the bottle!

MASTER MAGICIAN

CYRIL TAKAYAMA (born 1973)

Cyril Takayama was born in the United States but moved to Japan as a teenager to make a living doing street magic. Today he is a huge star in Japan. He does many big, glamorous **illusions** but also astounding close-up effects. In one street magic trick, he draws sunglasses on the face on a bill, makes the sunglasses move on to the forehead, and then magically rubs them off with a napkin. As a final touch, the napkin bursts into flames, transforming into a real pair of sunglasses, which Takayama puts on before strolling away.

Dice Magic

DICE FROM BOARD games make handy props for close-up magic as they are small and easy to handle. Some dice tricks use self-working methods that don't need sleight-of-hand, while others involve sneakier moves that require practice.

MATH MASTER

This smart self-working trick will make your friends think you have amazing math skills!

1. Boast about how sharp your mental math skills are and offer to prove it. Give a friend four dice and ask them to pile them in a tower. Turn your back so you can't see.

2. Say that you can figure out how many dots on the dice are hidden from view and add them up in five seconds flat. Now turn around and pretend to scan the dice. In fact, you only need to look at the number on the top die.

number on top die is 4

3. In your head, subtract the number you saw from 28. Pretend to be doing furious calculations, and then announce the total just before your five seconds are up.

28 – 4 = 24

24!

4. When your friends lift the dice and add all the dots on the hidden faces, they'll find you were exactly right!

$3 + 6 + 1 + 2 + 5 + 2 + 5 = 24$

Do this trick twice in case people think the answer is always the same.

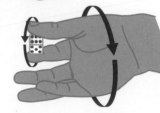
THE DISAPPEARING SPOT

This trick uses a sleight called the paddle move.
You give a die an extra twist so it turns more than people realize. The smaller the die, the easier this is.

1. Hold up a die like this, displaying one dot with the five dots on the top face, hidden under your index finger.

2. Flick your hand over to show the opposite face, which has six dots on it. Do this a couple of times.

3. Now say you'll make a dot disappear. Wave your other hand over the die, and turn your hand over again—but this time, turn the die around in your fingers as well, in the same direction as your hand is moving.

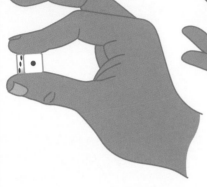

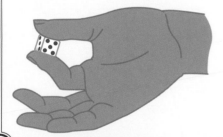

Roll the die over in your fingers as you turn your hand.

4. Because you've given the die an extra turn, the face now showing is the one with five spots, not six.

5. To "replace" the lost dot, turn the die back over in your fingers as you turn your hand to its original position. Now turn your hand over in the ordinary way so the six is visible again.

Let people see the die afterward, so they can check it's not a trick one.

MASTER MAGICIAN

JOHN SCARNE (1903–1985)

John Scarne first began learning tricks to become a gambling cheat, but his mom persuaded him to be a magician instead! Scarne performed on stage and also wrote many books on magic and games. As well as showing how to perform different sleights and self-working effects, he explained the rules of card and dice games and warned readers about methods used by **con men**. Can you guess how people might cheat with dice? Find the answer on page 32.

Cups and Balls

THE CUPS AND balls trick is one of the most famous close-up tricks of all time. It starts with one ball under each cup and ends with all the balls together as if they have jumped through the cups. The trick is hundreds of years old and has been performed by so many magicians that there are several thousand versions.

MAGICAL MOVES

Over the years, magicians have added their own twists to the cups and balls trick, such as making the balls disappear or change color or replacing them with other objects. One magician, called Johnny Ace Palmer, ended his routine by revealing live chicks under each cup.

GAZZO MACEE
(born 1960)

Gazzo Macee is an English street magic performer who is famous for his version of the cups and balls trick, which he turns into a long routine with lots of surprises. He finishes by lifting cups to reveal various fruits, such as melons, that are so big they don't even fit under the cups!

TRICK OF THE TRADE
Make sure the balls are all the same size and color and that you can't see through the cups.

CLASSIC CUPS AND BALLS
This version needs three cups and four balls.
You can buy these from magic shops or use everyday objects instead.

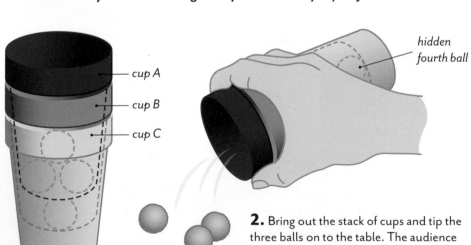

1. Before you perform, stack the three cups with one ball in the middle cup (cup B). Put the remaining three balls in the top cup (cup A).

Make sure the cups stack normally even with a ball in one of them.

cup A

cup B

cup C

hidden fourth ball

2. Bring out the stack of cups and tip the three balls on to the table. The audience doesn't know there's a hidden fourth ball.

3. Take each cup off the stack and turn it over on the table. Keep the tops of the cups facing you, and turn them quickly. This means that when you turn cup B, the hidden ball won't fall out or be seen.

hidden ball

Turn each cup in the same way so no one suspects there's a ball in cup B.

4. Place the balls in front of the cups. Then put the middle ball on top of cup B.

Audience view

5. Now cover the ball with cup A and cup C.

6. Tap the top of the cups, and then lift up the stack. It seems to the audience that the ball has gone through cup B and is now underneath it.

7. Pick up the stack and lay out the cups again as in step 3. The second cup in your stack (cup A) has a hidden ball in it. Put this cup over the ball that just appeared on the table.

8. Put a ball on top of cup A and cover it with cups B and C.

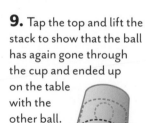

9. Tap the top and lift the stack to show that the ball has again gone through the cup and ended up on the table with the other ball.

10. Put the cups back on the table again as in steps 3 and 7. Again, the second cup (cup B) has a hidden ball in it. Put this cup over the two balls you just revealed.

11. Now put the last ball on top of cup B and cover it with A and C.

12. Tap the cups and lift the stack to show that all three balls are now together on the table!

Now put everything away, so no one discovers the fourth ball.

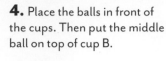

Rubber Bands

ALL YOU NEED for these close-up tricks are rubber bands and flexible fingers! Try using rubber bands of different lengths and thicknesses to see which work best for you.

THE JUMPING RUBBER BAND
This rubber band trick is easy and looks amazing.

1. Hold up your right hand, palm facing you, and put a rubber band over your index and middle fingers.

2. Tell the audience you can make the band jump. As you talk, stretch the band toward you with your left hand.

3. Curl up your right fingers and put them into the loop you've made. Then let go with your left hand.

The audience doesn't see this side.

4. Now say a magic word or snap your left fingers, and then quickly open your right hand. The band will jump on to your other two fingers!

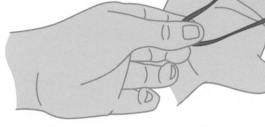

You can do the trick again and make the band jump back on to the first two fingers.

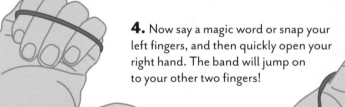

TRICK OF THE TRADE
Follow up by asking a volunteer to trap the band on your fingers by twisting a second, larger rubber band around your fingertips. When you do the trick, the band will still jump in exactly the same way!

20

Snap It and Swap It

This is a classic rubber band effect—you snap a band in half and then magically make it whole again. As an extra twist, you also make two bands change places!

1. Find two identical rubber bands. Snip one in half.

2. Hold the cut band in your finger and thumb so it looks whole. Show a volunteer both bands and ask them to point to one.

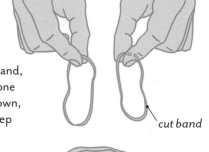

cut band

3. If they choose the cut band, say, "OK, this is yours." Put down the whole band and push the cut one into their hand, closing their fingers over it, so they don't see it's broken. Tell them to keep their hand out.

4. If they choose the whole band, say, "OK, this is the one we'll use." Put it down, and ask them to keep the other band in their hand as in step 3.

They always end up with the cut band!

5. While you're telling the volunteer to keep their hand out, pick up the whole band and stretch it out double, pinching it at both ends.

6. Quickly wrap the band around one hand and curl your fingers to hold the end in place underneath.

7. Stretch it, so it looks like one strand, not two. Twist it a few times as you stretch it.

Keep it taut, or people will see two strands.

8. Now say you'll break the band. Pull one end away with your index finger and thumb. The elastic will make a snapping noise.

9. Stretch it out to show it's "broken" with your hands covering the ends.

10. Quickly scrunch it into your hand and make a fist. Say that you can make the two bands swap places. Snap your fingers or say magic words.

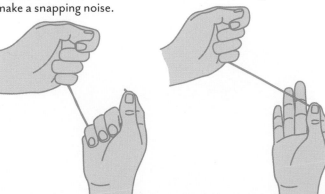

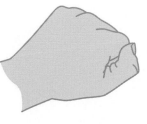

11. Open your hand slowly to reveal the whole band. Now ask the volunteer to open their hand. They'll be amazed to see their band is broken!

Amazing Matches

MATCHES MAKE USEFUL props for brilliant close-up effects, but remember they can be dangerous! Only do tricks with used matches. Alternatively, use toothpicks, as they work just as well.

BROKEN AND MENDED MATCH PART 1
This trick needs two used matches and a thick piece of cloth with a hem around it, such as a cloth napkin or bandanna.

1. Before you start, secretly push one match into the hem of the napkin.

2. Shake out the napkin to show it's empty. Then lay it on the table. Make sure you know where the hidden match is. Place the second match in the middle of the napkin.

hidden match

3. Fold over the four corners of the napkin to cover the match. Make sure the hidden match is near the second match, and remember its position.

Remember where you place this corner.

4. Pick up the bundle and hold the hidden match through the material. Your audience thinks this is the match you wrapped up. Ask someone to feel it to make sure it's there.

hidden match
second match here

5. Now ask the person to break the match through the cloth.

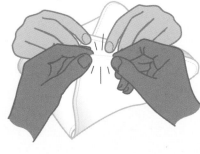

6. Put the napkin back on the table and wave your hands over it or snap your fingers. Slowly unfold the corners to reveal the match, miraculously whole again.

broken match hidden here

BROKEN AND MENDED MATCH PART 2

Here's a great follow-up. You can use the same napkin, but find an extra match.

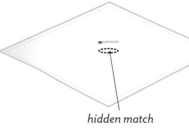

TRICK OF THE TRADE
Make sure your napkin is thick, so the hidden match doesn't show underneath. It must have the same pattern on both sides, or people will realize that you unrolled it a different way!

1. First, sneakily place a whole match on the table and cover it with the napkin in this position.

hidden match

2. Take the whole match from the previous trick and say, "OK, let's try this again—break the match again for me, please!"

3. Place the broken match on the napkin. Make sure it's higher than your hidden match.

hidden match

4. Now grab a wedge of cloth which contains both the broken match and the hidden one, and start rolling it away from you.

top section

bottom section

The bottom section of the napkin is bigger than the top section.

5. When you've rolled it all up, flip over the uppermost corner and lay it flat on the table.

The bottom corner now looks like the top corner.

6. Hold the two corners and pull them apart to reveal the whole match!

Sweep everything onto your lap quickly so no one sees the broken match.

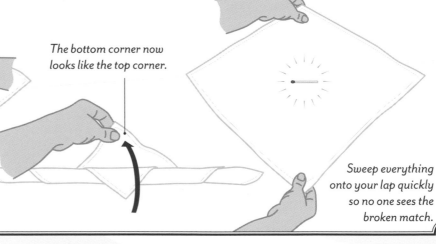

MASTER MAGICIAN

NATE LEIPZIG (1873–1939)

The Swedish magician Nate Leipzig was a big fan of tricks with small, everyday objects such as matches. He began his career by borrowing magic props from another magician and performing big illusions on stage, but he felt frustrated—he was good, but his props often let him down by being clunky and unreliable. Then he discovered card magic and realized that small, gracefully-performed sleights could be far more amazing to an audience than over-the-top stage effects. He went on to create his own clever close-up tricks, which he performed to audiences around the world.

Mealtime Magic

MANY CLOSE-UP MAGICIANS perform in restaurants. The setting is perfect with a table, a ready-made audience, and useful props, such as napkins and toothpicks. Try these tricks using glasses and cups at the dinner table.

THE THREE-GLASS PUZZLE

Here's a quick riddle to start your routine. You need three identical glasses or cups.

1. Challenge a friend to turn three glasses the right way up in just three moves, turning two glasses each time. As you talk, put the glasses upside down and turn the middle one upright.

2. Quickly show them how it's done. Turn the first and second glasses so they look like this.

3. Then turn the first and third, so they look like this.

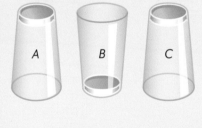

4. Then turn the first and second, so they're all the right way up.

5. Now it's your friend's turn. Set up the glasses again, turning the middle glass upside down. Your friend won't notice the starting position is different . . . and they won't solve the puzzle either!

THE MAGICAL MELTING GLASS

The key to this trick is misdirection—everyone thinks you're doing magic with a coin, so no one pays attention to the glass!

1. Announce that you can make a coin melt through the table. Place a coin in front of you and put a small glass or cup upside down on it.

2. Drape a paper napkin over the glass and press it in place with your hands so it is molded to the shape of the glass.

3. Hold the napkin and glass with one hand and pretend to concentrate on making the coin melt through the table.

4. With a flourish, lift up the glass and napkin and move them to the edge of the table. Exclaim, "What? It's still there!" While everyone is focused on the coin, gently let the glass fall out of the napkin on to your lap.

?!

Don't look at the glass or napkin!

5. Act embarrassed. Say, "Sorry everyone . . . I'll try again." Hold the napkin gently, so you don't crush the shape, and put it back over the coin.

empty napkin over coin

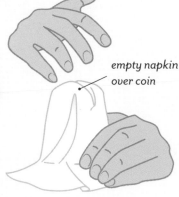

6. Pretend to concentrate again, and lift the napkin away again. Appear amazed that the coin is still there!

I just don't understand it!

7. Say, "OK, I'll try one more time." Close your eyes and screw up your face in concentration. Then suddenly slap one hand down on top of the napkin, squashing it flat on the table.

8. With your other hand, take the glass from your lap and hold it up.

Wow, I concentrated so hard I made the glass melt through the table instead!

TRICK OF THE TRADE
For a more dramatic effect, use a plastic cup so you can open your legs and let the cup clatter to the floor, as though it went through the table.

Fun with Food

IF YOU'RE PERFORMING magic at a dinner table, in a restaurant, or at a party, try food magic, too! Here are some quick food tricks to make everyone laugh.

READY-SLICED BANANA

1. Beforehand, carefully push a toothpick through the skin of a banana. Move it from side to side so it cuts through the banana without breaking the skin.

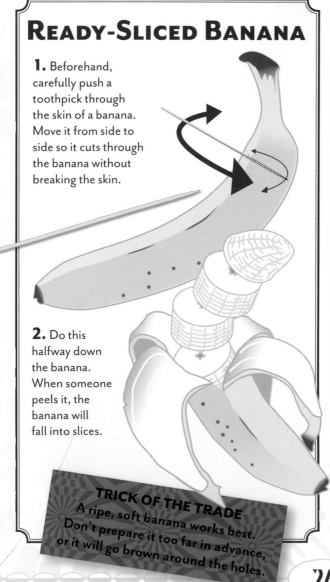

2. Do this halfway down the banana. When someone peels it, the banana will fall into slices.

TRICK OF THE TRADE
A ripe, soft banana works best. Don't prepare it too far in advance, or it will go brown around the holes.

GREAT GRAPE BALANCE

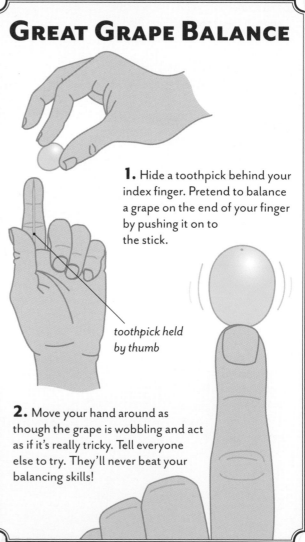

1. Hide a toothpick behind your index finger. Pretend to balance a grape on the end of your finger by pushing it on to the stick.

toothpick held by thumb

2. Move your hand around as though the grape is wobbling and act as if it's really tricky. Tell everyone else to try. They'll never beat your balancing skills!

THE MAGIC FINGER

Can you figure out why this trick works? Go to page 32 to find out.

1. Secretly go to the bathroom and put a smear of liquid soap on the tip of your index finger.

2. At the table, sprinkle pepper all over the surface of a small bowl of water. Tell everyone that magicians have magical fingers and offer to prove it.

3. Ask someone to dip a finger into the bowl. Nothing happens. When you try with your soapy finger, the pepper shoots away to the sides of the bowl!

THE BALANCING EGG

Use a raw egg for this trick.

1. When no one is watching, pour a small pile of salt on the table in front of you—less than a teaspoon will do.

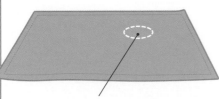

Remember where the salt is.

2. Spread your napkin over the top. Show the egg and challenge people to balance it on its end. Suggest they spread out their napkins first, like you, in case it breaks.

3. After everyone has tried and failed, place the egg carefully on top of the salt. When you're sure it's steady, say a magic word, or snap the fingers of your other hand and let go. The egg stays upright!

FRED KAPS

(1926–1980)

Fred Kaps was a skilled sleight-of-hand magician and a great performer. His most famous trick used salt. As music played, Kaps emptied a salt shaker into his fist. He opened his hand and it was empty, but then he closed it again and salt came pouring out. He refilled the salt shaker, the music stopped, and people clapped—but salt still poured from his fist. While the audience laughed, Kaps pretended to panic as the salt kept flowing. He gestured to the band to play on as he tried to scoop handfuls into his pockets. By the end of the routine, there was salt all over the stage. Kaps worked on this trick for three years, during which his living room was constantly covered in salt!

Show Time!

ONCE YOU'VE LEARNED a few close-up tricks and practiced until you can do them well, pack your props into your pockets and head out to impress your friends. Don't be tempted to tell them how you do tricks even if they beg you, or you'll spoil the fun!

OK, the comedy show's over . . . now I'll start on the magic!

If you crack a joke, the audience won't care that you made a mistake—they'll be too busy enjoying themselves.

DISASTER!

It can happen to any magician—you drop a prop or fumble a sleight, and your trick is in ruins. Don't panic or apologize. Laugh it off and swiftly move on to your next trick, or do something different with the same prop. It's always useful to know more tricks than you plan to perform, just in case you need to throw in an extra one!

TRICK OF THE TRADE

Get your timing right. Don't start tricks at the table when people are eating or if food is arriving. Wait until you're sure you won't be interrupted. If in doubt, save your trick for another time.

GO WITH THE FLOW

Never force your audience to sit and watch trick after trick. Be spontaneous—for example, if you're waiting at a bus stop, there might be time for a couple of coin or rubber band tricks. Be flexible, too—for example, if you'd planned to do the Magical Melting Glass (page 25), but there are no paper napkins, perform something else instead.

EYE-CATCHING EFFECTS

Try learning a few fancy hand flourishes to make your tricks look more professional. Here are a couple to practice.

To display a pack of cards, hold them in one hand and spread them evenly across the table.

With your other hand, flick the end card faceup, so that the rest of the cards flip over in a ripple effect.

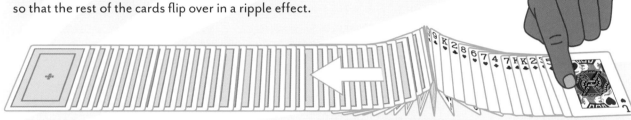

When you bring out a coin, place it on the back of your hand and hold your hand out straight.

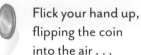

Flick your hand up, flipping the coin into the air . . .

. . . then grab the coin.

MASTER MAGICIAN

JEFF SHERIDAN (born 1948)

Jeff Sheridan is an American magician famous for his imaginative performance style. He began his career in Central Park, New York, where he did amazing card tricks and flourishes mostly in silence. He went on to form a theater group which used dance and magic to create weird and wonderful shows. He is also an inventor of magic products.

Glossary

con men
short for confidence men; people who appear to be honest, but in fact cheat others out of money

cut
to take a chunk of cards from the top of a facedown pile, put them on the table, and then place the rest of the pile on top

deck
a full set or pack of playing cards

flourish
a fancy or showy move that makes a trick look more impressive

gimmick
a secret part or object—for example, a false bottom or hidden spring that makes a trick work

illusion
an effect that tricks you into thinking something impossible is happening; Famous magical illusions include sawing someone in half and making objects float in the air.

misdirection
the skill of drawing people's attention away from something you don't want them to see or think too much about

palm
to hide a card in the palm of your hand so it can't be seen

patter
prepared, practiced speech that magicians use when performing magic tricks; Although you need to work out your patter beforehand, make sure you speak naturally and don't read it out like a script.

prop
short for property; any object that is used to help perform a trick

shuffle
to mix up a deck of cards in your hands

sleight-of-hand
the technique of secretly moving, altering, or swapping objects to create a magical effect; Sleights (pronounced "slights") take a lot of practice to perform well and also rely on good misdirection skills.

street magic
magic tricks that are performed outside, often for small groups of people who gather around the magician to watch

Web Sites

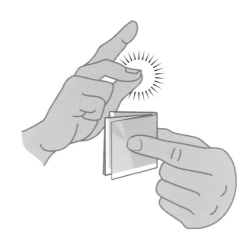

www.magictricks.com/library
Read biographies of famous magicians and discover fascinating facts about
their lives and the tricks they invented.

www.activitytv.com/magic-tricks-for-kids
Find great videos that show you how to perform some of the close-up tricks in
this book, plus many more. Search for tricks by skill level, or browse them all.

www.oldandsold.com/articles02/magictricks12.shtml
Read lots of inventive ideas for tricks to do at the dinner table using food,
cutlery, and glasses.

www.videojug.com/film/how-to-perform-the-cup-and-balls-trick
Watch a useful video that takes you through the stages of the famous cups
and balls trick as shown on pages 18 and 19.

www.magicsam.com/index.asp
Find out about The Society of American Magicians, the oldest magical society in
the world, which was once headed by Harry Houdini. Read about recent magic
news and find S. A. M. assemblies in your area!

www.magician.org/
Learn about the history of the International Brotherhood of Magicians, the world's
largest organization for those interested in or practicing magic. Find magic shows,
lectures, and conventions near you!

Index

bills 5, 14–15

cards 4, 5, 7, 8–9, 17, 23, 29
chicks 18
coins 5, 7, 10–11, 12–13, 15, 25, 28, 29
con men 17
cups and balls 18–19
cutting cards 8

dice 5, 16–17, 32

flourishes 7, 29
food 5, 12, 26–27, 28

gimmicks 5
glasses 24, 25
guerilla magic 4

magicians
  Downs, Thomas Nelson 13
  Kaps, Fred 27
  Leipzig, Nate 23
  Macee, Gazzo 18
  Malini, Max 7
  Palmer, Johnny Ace 18

Scarne, John 17
Sheridan, Jeff 29
Slydini, Tony 5
Takayama, Cyril 15
matches 5, 6, 22–23
misdirection 6, 7, 12, 25

napkins 5, 15, 22, 23, 24, 25, 27, 28

paddle move 17
palming 7, 12, 13
paper clips 7
patter 6
performance tips 7, 28–29
props 4, 5, 7, 10, 16, 22, 23, 24, 28

rubber bands 5, 20–21, 28

shuffling 8
sleight-of-hand 5, 7, 12, 13, 16, 17, 23, 27, 28
soap 27, 32
street magic 4, 15, 18

toothpicks 22, 24, 26
tricks
  The Balancing Egg 27
  Bread Roll Surprise 12
  Broken and Mended Match 22–23
  Classic Cups and Balls 18–19
  The Disappearing Spot 17
  Great Grape Balance 26
  Jumping Coins 11
  Jumping Jacks 9
  The Jumping Rubber Band 20
  The Magic Finger 27
  Magic Linking Paper Clips 7
  The Magical Melting Glass 25
  Math Master 16
  Multiply Your Money 13
  Ready-Sliced Banana 26
  The Shrinking Coin 10
  Snap It and Swap It 21
  The Three-Glass Puzzle 24
  The Trapped Bill 15
  Turning Money on its Head 14
  X-Ray Vision 11

wands 7

SECRETS OF MAGIC ... REVEALED!

Page 17: How might people cheat with dice?

Answer: They use loaded dice, which can be altered so they are more likely to land with a certain face showing. There are many ways of altering a die, including rounding some edges, putting weights inside, or filling it with wax, which melts when warmed and drips into a hollow, making that part heavier. One type of loaded die has a magnet inside, which is attracted to a coil of wire built into the game table!

Page 27: How does The Magic Finger trick work?

Answer: This trick works because the pepper floats on a very thin film of water on the surface. The soap breaks this film, making it pull back to the sides of the bowl and taking the pepper with it.